Quiet Spaces

Quiet Spaces

William Smalley

foreword   Edmund de Waal

photography   Harry Crowder

Hélène Binet

Contents

Edmund de Waal

More than Enough

I always wanted to be an architect. My childhood was spent in rambling medieval houses in the shadows of two great cathedrals – Lincoln until the age of twelve and then Canterbury. They were buildings that had not been planned – spiral staircases, corridors and blocked doors, grandeur and the patched-up in juxtaposition. And all in sight and sound of cathedrals: the way back from school was through the cloisters and bells rang a curfew at nine every night. I once gave a lecture on the oddness of this upbringing and called it 'On Being Very Cold', a nod to waking up to frosty bedrooms. But the coldness of living in houses with no central heating was in part an austerity, a pared-back quality of being sheltered in places where there were other, slower and deeper concerns. These places had a longer life. These were houses with stone steps that had become gently scalloped, banisters burnished by thousands of iterative movements, windows where the leaded glass rippled. And there were the marks of how these buildings had been created: these were places 'known and handled', to borrow the words of the poet and artist David Jones. And as a child I found windowsills and the turns of staircases to curl up on and read, those liminal spaces where you hide, turned inwards into words, turned outwards as you watch light change.

In becoming a potter I'm still trying to find those particular places where the world knits itself together, the places where you actually want to be. And then my practice is to put something down – a group of vessels on a shelf, some porcelain in a vitrine – and see

Arcanum *in Edmund's studio, made for his Kettle's Yard show of 2005*

how that minute quantum of energy changes, articulates and catches shadows, reflects. And pauses the huge velocity of the world, the tear-it-up, move-it-on speed.

This lambent book is a meditation on time. It is a series of pauses in particular buildings. Alongside his own spaces, William has chosen houses and artists' studios, an art gallery in the country, the private spaces of architects and potters and families. What threads them together is his personal philosophy that quietness is not really about good taste at all, more a rather astringent exercise in balancing objects and sight lines, an attempt to find correspondences between the made and the found. His feeling for the kindness of materials shines through. You want to touch.

This reminds me of the Cistercian writer and hermit Thomas Merton's photographs of the woods and barns around his hermitage: a way of bringing a focus on to the quotidian. After visiting Pleasant Hill, the Shaker community in Kentucky, in 1961 and 1962, he wrote of 'marvelous, silent, vast spaces around the old buildings. Cold, pure light ... How the blank side of a frame house can be so completely beautiful I cannot imagine. A completely miraculous achievement of forms.' He found that the Shakers' attentiveness to how to live fully in the material world was reflected in the care they took with the disposition of objects, the positioning of a window, the construction of a chair: 'The peculiar grace of a Shaker chair is due to the fact that it was made by someone capable of believing that an angel might come and sit on it.'

So here we have a beautiful book of places. Some I have known all my life, some I have been lucky enough to make work for. Many are new to me. But what this carefully paced book does is to walk me into different spaces, let me sit and inhabit one possibility of becoming quieter and then another. It is in praise of shadows. That is enough, I want to say. That is more than enough.

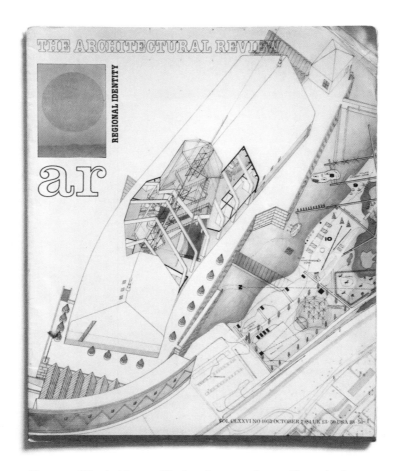

The copy of The Architectural Review *given to me by my village school headmaster when I was ten*

Quietude

I am writing this to music. Murray Perahia playing Bach's partitas. The room is not silent, there is noise. My dog is sighing in his sleep beside me. The noise of the street outside comes in through the windows. The room is a mix of stuff: my grandfather's Georgian college table, a piano a year older than me, the oarlock of a Venetian gondola, various chairs, books to be read and filed. The room itself is also a mix, built in the eighteenth century, re-fronted in the nineteenth century, the floor raised in the twentieth, with panelling that turned out to be modern when I stripped and painted it white a decade ago. It could be an incoherent mess, but the light is the same light that has been falling through the windows since it was built, and, perhaps because everything inside is from my eye, there is, to me, peace. I am able to think. It is quiet.

To be quiet is not to be silent, and quiet spaces are not empty. Emptiness can be oppressive.

I like the quiet passages in music. I have been lost in music dancing in the middle of a club, the effect a near-silence, but equally I have been transported by one or two people on a stage singing, their voices nonetheless filling the concert hall, or by a few instruments playing together in intense conversation. If a chorus comes on stage, or when an orchestra is in full flight, I tend to switch off, looking for fake conversations at the back. Fakeness always bothers me, disturbs my sense of peace.

Growing up, I was a quiet boy, content to observe and draw. One evening when I was about eight I came down to the kitchen to find a handsome man sitting at the table: 'This is our architect,' said my mother, and looking at his plans for an extension to our house, I knew that that was what I wanted to do. At my village school I spent all my lunchtimes and games lessons designing houses.

The Uffington White Horse, photographed by Paul Nash around 1937

The headmaster, Michael Armstrong, an extraordinary teacher who happened to have landed in our village, bought me a copy of *The Architectural Review* when I was ten. I still have it. A few years ago, having seen an article about my flat, he sent me an email saying that he could see an intuitive thread connecting the drawings I made in his class when I was ten and eleven, and my work now. These were amazing words to receive. I have come to realize the importance of intuition in design, as in life, and I work hard to keep in touch with my intuitive self.

Perhaps since I am by nature quiet, as an architect my intuitive response to a site is to seek the quiet response. Not the most invisible, but one that achieves a state of quietude through being right. The Oxfordshire Farm shown here [pp. 60–71] is bold; a new extension twisting to link the existing farmhouse with a barn alongside, but I think it has a quietude through a sense of rightness, through an instinctive response to the particular requirements of the client and the particularities of the site, and through a use of materials that over time have weathered to harmonize with the existing stone walls and slate roofs. That rightness cannot be achieved rationally. An element of inspiration is required.

My favourite work of art is the Uffington White Horse, near where I grew up. It is thought to be around three thousand years old, yet the abstracted figure of the horse cut into the turf on a chalk escarpment could be by Barbara Hepworth [pp. 72–83] or Henry Moore, and the way it leaps over the head of the folding valley below, commanding a view of all of Oxfordshire beyond, is still powerful today. It feels inevitable. Through simple means, its quiet presence belies its power. My architecture seeks to touch the same qualities of inevitability, strength and elegance.

Architecture school in the 1990s in Edinburgh was at the tail end of modernism, the final years of the last tutors on permanent tenure from the 1960s, stuck at Aalto and unable to move, or be moved, on. When you see the overwrought classical buildings of the early twentieth century, you realise why modernism had to happen, but for all the truth to materials, the modern movement was based on a falsehood, the assumption of rationality – Le Corbusier's houses as 'machines for living in'. Architecture responds to emotional needs. There is no purely rational architecture, and the best modernist buildings are eccentric works of genius. And modernism's concept of universal space, your piece defined with the minimum of means, feels to me cold and impersonal. I remember standing in the entrance of Mies van der Rohe's Neue Nationalgalerie in Berlin, its neon-lit space seeming to continue identically in all directions, and being freaked out by the uniformity. It felt like a dystopia. There are no shadows, and there is nowhere to hide in modernism. And sometimes we all need to hide.

Soft limewash walls in Roger Capps's hall house in the Welsh borders, where I worked as a conservation builder when a student

The new buildings the younger tutors suggested we look at held little appeal to me, made of non-materials that would look best the day they were installed, and then begin a life of slow decline. I found myself more interested in old limewashed buildings, and when we had to go and work in practice for a year, I figured there would be time to sit at a drawing board later, and went on a search for materiality to work for a conservation builder, Roger Capps, having seen his old hall house in the Welsh borders in *The World of Interiors*, to carve beams for Windsor Castle and stone for Hereford Cathedral. Arriving to meet him at the house the evening before I started, and finding a note that he was out and to let myself in through the open door, I still remember the tall rooms whose ceilings were so high they were out of sight, the soft limewashed walls, and the late September light pouring down a panelled staircase. I thought it was, and perhaps still is, the most beautiful space I had ever been in.

Architecture students weren't supposed to like old limewashed rooms, or read *World of Interiors* – or, I think, be interested in comfort, in what it felt like to be in a space, to feel its pressures and presence. The house I grew up in – to which we moved on my third birthday, as if it was a present to me – was an old timber-framed weaver's house, in part fifteenth-century. Its fireplaces you could sit in, doors you had to duck under, crooked floors, and weavers' rooms in the attic you could hide in, taught me that spaces hold emotions and allow for our moods. And perhaps its age taught me not to think of history in terms of old and new, but as a continuum, in which human feeling is the constant. We all dream. Perhaps as a result too, my dreams have always been of houses.

Architectural space was much talked about in Edinburgh, but, at least by me, little understood, and it wasn't until I left that I began to understand what it meant. It is a modern concept. Classical architecture is concerned with representing mass through an ordered system, so that you notice the walls rather than what they contain. To me classical architecture feels spatial only when the orders are removed and it is stripped back to reveal pure mass. Its order appeals to my mathematical mind, but I find classical architecture's symmetry intrusively insistent. Architecture shouldn't be solely intellectual. It should appeal to the experiential soul. Classical churches rarely move me. They come from the wisdom of man, not the madness of the gods; to me they lack the awe of the unknown. Architectural space is experienced, is felt.

For a while I thought minimalism proposed a better way of being, and though I still favour less rather than more, I came to realize that it does not allow for life, for the human condition. The travel writer Bruce Chatwin wrote that surrounded by bare walls you can travel anywhere in your mind, but, unlike Chatwin, we can't always be elsewhere. Sometimes we need to feel at home. I went to a talk by the Belgian architect Vincent Van Duysen in which he said: We are all vulnerable.

A presentation painting for a visitor centre in the Outer Hebrides off the far coast of Scotland, from my third year of architecture studies

I thought it was such a beautiful thing to say, to acknowledge as an architect. Modernism failed to acknowledge our vulnerability.

Architectural studies are lengthy, but beyond trying out and discarding ideas, what I took away was the sense of a building achieving resolution. This was much discussed, but little explained, as if an initiation test. It was something I think we were supposed to intuit, and in the end did; the sense of a perfect response, one of any number of perfect responses, in which everything adds to the whole. When the brief has been understood, when nothing architectural can be added or removed except for the worse, when the design flows and becomes easy, the process feels like revealing an answer that was always there, waiting to be shown, like scraping back soil to reveal a white horse.

As students, we were obsessed to the point of block with representation, which, for me, I think reflected an impatience for the real thing, to build, an acknowledgment that drawings could never describe a space adequately, what it would feel like to be in it. A friend said of my projects, 'You can smell your buildings', which were about the only words I took away with me.

I still struggle with how to represent projects, short of building them. It is why when designing in the studio we work with physical models, to investigate and convey not the buildings themselves but the experience of being in them. Because when built, how you feel in a space is what is important. And, then, I prefer photographs that seek to express what it feels like to be in the space, rather than to explain it. The best spaces to be in are not always those that photograph best. They are not designed to be shown, but for the experience of being in them. The way light falls through the day, the tactility, the temporal qualities of the materials they are built with. In such a space details become important. It is as happy to be alone as with company, and music flows in such spaces.

It takes a quiet confidence to be an architect, a confidence born of an inner resolve. But a modesty is also required, the humility to know that the life that goes on in a space is greater than the space itself.

When I hand over a project it is for the client to begin to fill it with life. I think it is a test of good architecture that it can take objects of any period and they feel good, the space feels better. I find interiors that are full of only old or new things eerie. The architecture I respond to shares qualities with writers' or artists' studios, spaces designed for creativity. There is an openness that comes with the openness with which they were designed. When they are right, the best spaces achieve a peace, and take personal expression through the possessions put in them.

It is through the quietude of being right that a space becomes alive. This is an elusive quality, but is one that feels settled, inevitable. This is quiet space.

Space

Space

I was perhaps first conscious of space standing in a garden, when I was about five or six, visiting a great-aunt in the New Forest. I remember standing between hedges in her garden and being aware of the sense of enclosure.

I spent much of my childhood looking at pictures of buildings and trying to work out their plans. But perhaps an understanding of architectural space came through the one I was actually in: our family home, a fifteenth-century weaver's house, which had sloping floors you had to arrange the furniture by, fireplaces you could sit inside and attic rooms you could retreat to when you needed to be alone. It seemed to reflect us all, and its spaces held my emotions.

Going through architecture school, space was much discussed but little understood, by me at least. Architecture students are told to read *The Poetics of Space* by Gaston Bachelard, a dry book that occasionally allows itself great moments of poetry, and which only made sense to me later, when my emotions had developed. Bachelard, a French philosopher, explains the psyche through the medium of the house: the cellar as repository of memory, the attic as place to dream. His book reveals the allusive power of architectural space, and how we relate to it emotionally, in terms other than purely rational.

It was only once I'd finished my studies, and was working on my own projects, and felt free, that I think I began to get a true sense of the space contained in a building as plastic, malleable; and of the ability to play with the space contained as much as its container.

Essentially space is what is contained between walls. Classical architecture was concerned with the walls and the expression of their mass; modernism the opposite: the minimum mass required to define your piece of a uniform, universal space. The Pantheon in Rome, constructed almost two thousand years ago, is for me the greatest architectural space, a semispherical dome, its open oculus casting a moving shaft of light through the interior (if it rains in Rome, go and watch the rain falling as if in slow motion through the space). Mies van der Rohe's Barcelona Pavilion, built for the International Exposition in 1929 (demounted after but reconstructed in 1986), is perhaps the purest expression of modern space, its perfect roof plane floating over screens of onyx and travertine stone, the space beneath unenclosed (like the Pantheon it is open to the elements), and so free that my niece took her first steps when we were there.

Air moves on, but space remains. It should be easy to describe, but the more I consider it, the more difficult to pin down it becomes. Soon I want to describe how it makes me feel to be in it, to experience it, and feelings are not easy to set down.

Great spaces as the Pantheon and Barcelona Pavilion are, they are both spaces to visit, not to inhabit. They provide for only one emotion: awe, and we are more complicated than that, are vulnerable, and need to be held by our spaces. This is what my crooked childhood house taught me: that space is emotional, and has to be experienced. It exists in our minds and in our memories.

Though the physicality of what defines or contains the space is not irrelevant. If the walls are solid or glazed, openings are deep or a roof as elegantly thin as possible, whether surfaces are warm timber or cool stone, rough or polished smooth, all affect the feeling of being in a space.

But beyond the physical, architectural space can feel that it flows fluidly, or be held in the containment of a nook. It can soar, and it can compress. It can provide a place to play the piano or take your first steps, can encourage a convivial meal, be a place to appreciate art or enjoy music. Architecture, through the spaces it creates, can elate, can comfort, can protect. Architects have the power to carve emotion in space and to provide places for our emotions.

Space is an experience, a feeling. Space is how a building makes you feel. Architecture is how you feel in it.

London Modernism

London UK 2020

When the clients first showed me photos of this 1950s modernist courtyard house in southwest London, with its sense of openness and floor-to-ceiling glass, I remember thinking: Why don't we all live like this? They were buying it from the children of the couple who had commissioned it from architect Leslie Gooday in 1958, who had extended it a few years later but otherwise more or less kept it in its original state.

The house has a reticence, hidden by planting from the street. It reveals itself in layers. Our work involved opening up views through the house that were originally oddly curtailed; the central corridor between the bedroom block at the front and living block at the rear was doubled in width to give a sense of ease, the kitchen formed from service rooms.

Climbing up on to the flat roof on the first visit to see what state it was in brought memories of my village school, whose roof I had produced a measured survey of when I was ten or eleven. It also revealed a view out into the trees of the protected common opposite. It seemed clear that this was the view you would want to wake up to, and so now the master bedroom forms a new upper floor to the previously single-storey house, with a picture window looking straight out from the bed into the tree canopy. The bedroom is accessed up a new semicircular staircase wrapping around a solid wood totem pole that sits below a circular skylight above, so that it supports only the sky.

34   *The new first floor extension seen from the common opposite*

Otherwise it was a project of careful conservation – cork tiles relaid to the original rectangular grid, teak window frames replacing the original painted wood, insulation under newly laid copper sheets on the roof as the original drawings showed had been intended, but never enacted. Newly built elements are constructed in timber and faced with hardwood cladding to subtly differentiate them. The cork floor seems to flow through the house, like the garden between and beyond.

Though built in a time of austerity, and clearly with a sense of economy, the house has a complex plan and the quantity of windows is great for its size. The complexity gives views between rooms and across courtyards, making simply walking through the house, in the morning, through the day, or to bed, an uplifting journey.

It is a house everyone passing seems warmly envious of – for its openness, its light, and its open relationship with the courtyards and garden – and I think also for the spirit of optimism promised by its modernism that it has managed to hold on to.

36   *The entrance with the first of the house's courtyards beyond*

38–39   *Dappled light falls in the central corridor*

40   *The dining room at the rear of the kitchen opens out to the garden*

41   *The kitchen cupboards and island were designed for the house*

42   *A totem pole rises in the centre of the new stair, topped by a skylight*

43   *A corner of the new master bedroom. The walls are lined in olive-green linen*

44–45   *The master bedroom picture window overlooking the common*

Luis Barragán

Casa Barragán

Mexico City Mexico 1948–1988

Mexican architect Luis Barragán's own house, in an unassuming street in a quiet area of Mexico City, was created over forty years of experimentation.

It doesn't follow any standard model for how a house should be. Barragán was single, and though it is large, this is a house for one particular person. He bought the site foremost for the garden, now overgrown to the point of wildness. A dark and low timber-boarded entrance lobby with rough stone floor leads straight off the street, and up a few steps to the central stair hall. Side light falls down the stairwell over a Mathias Goeritz gold-leaf painting. The solid stair leads up to the side and back.

Deep reveals lead ahead to a modest dining room and intimate breakfast room, or, through a low door, into the main space: a living room, library and galleried music room, an extravagantly generous space occupying half the house's volume. The ceiling soars above. Below, the floor changes from pine boards at the rear to fitted carpet at the front, giving a plushly restrained quiet in the more intimate library. Low walls and shelving divide the space, with the living room and the famous cruciform window in its deep reveal looking into the garden at the rear, and an abstract, milky gridded window raised over the library and street at the front. The cantilevered timber stair, inspired by traditional Mexican barn stairs, leads to a further private study, galleried over the library but concealed behind a screen wall. Though a large space, it is a space to be alone in. It doesn't feel set

up for sociability. Throughout the house walls are in rough plaster, whitewashed or brightest pink, the texture holding the light and giving depth, the colour giving intense luminosity to the spaces. The main stair leads past guest bedrooms to Barragán's private rooms, places of refuge and retreat at the back overlooking the garden, and on through a narrow opening to a hidden stair up to the roof.

Though it unfolds in unexpected ways, if there is a repeated theme it is of small, almost secret doorways and passages leading into large spaces, or into courtyards open to the sky, so that as you enter, having come through, you automatically look upwards. The house hovers between enclosure and airy openness, containment and spatial freedom.

It is hard to imagine the spaces without Barragán's possessions, his low sofas and tables, lamps with stitched vellum shades, artworks, paintings and ceramics, and silver-glass balls – it would feel bare and empty without them.

As an architect, I can look at the plan of a house and imagine its spaces. But with Barragán's work that doesn't readily happen. His plans are deceptively simple. Yet made three-dimensional form, the spaces soar, interconnect, look past, through and over each other in ways not apparent from the two-dimensional drawing. It is disconcerting. But it makes his architecture endlessly fascinating and intriguing, unexpected and unique. Of spaces, above all, to be experienced, for long periods.

48   *Wooden boarded walls and bench, and blocks of rough-hewn stone on the floor in the entrance hall*

50–51   *Solid stone treads of the main stair lead to the sidelit open landing under a gold-leaf painting by Mathias Goeritz*

52–53   *Filtered garden light falls on the pine floorboards and rough-plastered walls of the main living room*

54–55   *Pots, books and low lamps provide intimacy in the library*

56   *The beamed ceiling soars over the living and library spaces*

57   *The famous cantilevered stair leading to the music gallery was inspired by traditional Mexican architecture*

Oxfordshire Farm

Oxfordshire UK 2011 & 2014
with James Gorst Architects

This farmhouse sits surrounded by its farm in Oxfordshire, having been home to the client's family who have farmed the land for well over half a century. The project, constructed in two phases to enable continuous oversight of the farm, spanned a decade; it was designed when I worked in James Gorst's studio and completed as a collaboration between our two offices.

At first one is conscious of the space of the wildflower meadow, created after 2 acres (about a hectare) of concrete farmyard were broken up and used as ballast for the new driveway that now crosses it. This leads to a new building with an open carport, and offices with a guest flat over alongside, on the site and following the form of an earlier barn that was built on unsure ground and demolished in the 1970s. This reinstated the original farmyard, now enclosed on three sides around a venerable apple tree, with the farmhouse beyond, and approached through timber-slatted gates, with something of the feel of a monastic quadrangle. The furthest barn has been simply converted as a painting studio. A stream flows beyond.

The path leads to the house's new entrance, opening into a hall in the space between the original farmhouse and a barn alongside, linking them to form one long house: a house of spaces leading one into the next, separated by gable walls and the farmhouse's two massive chimney stacks, but connected by a floor of Yorkstone slabs flowing between.

The hall leads through to a kitchen behind, angled to frame a view to the ford that crosses the lane outside, and round to the dramatic new stairwell, its landing cantilevered over over a glazed opening below, with a door to the master bedroom. A small winding stair leads on to two further bedrooms on the top floor. The former barn end of the house has an informal living room with a guest suite above. The upper floors and all joinery are in European oak. Rubblestone walls were insulated internally with a vermiculite and lime render, so that they retain their solidity and breathability. All walls and ceilings are finished in untinted, natural limewash.

The soft curve of the lime-plastered ceiling joins the new spaces of hall and stairwell as they wrap around the back of the house. The twisting external form stitches together the taller farmhouse and lower barn. Its stepped oak gives the cladding the mass of stone, and, left untreated, with the in-situ concrete, slate and lead roofs and warm grey rubblestone walls, forms a unified material palette tying old and new together. The horizontal slats of the cladding are repeated on the courtyard side to form a sunscreen shading the hall, through which climbing plants are growing so that house and barn are united into one.

You feel the space of the farm, meadow, courtyard and house. Space flows like time here. The constant running through is the simple spirit of the farm, and the unwavering commitment of the owners to it.

62   *The new stair at the rear of the house looking down towards the hall*

64–65   *The house's new entrance. The hall sits between the original farmhouse on the right and a barn, in what was the entrance to the yard*

66   *Looking up the new stair and along a newly created axis through the study to the drawing room beyond*

67   *Light and a sculpture on the cantilevered landing*

68–69   *The new kitchen and staircase extension seen from the lane*

70   *New and old meet at the back door*

71   *An external stone stair leads to guest accommodation in the new courtyard building*

Barbara Hepworth

Sculpture Garden

St Ives Cornwall UK 1949–1975

Barbara Hepworth's garden is small, a quarter of an acre (1,000 square metres), in the town of St Ives in furthest Cornwall, held aloft by huge retaining walls on three sides. It has the particular magic of walled gardens: of containment and surprise, experience condensed. Luis Barragán wrote that a perfect garden, no matter its size, should enclose nothing less than the entire universe, and for Hepworth there is the feeling that for her it did: that though she thought epically, this small garden was world enough.

It was extravagantly won at auction in 1949 for all the money Hepworth had, bidding against the council who wanted it for a car park, and she immediately recognized that it would be her place of nourishment. It was always about the garden and the three studios, greenhouses originally, that fall down the hill against the street wall, rather than the house, once a games room at the bottom of the former owner's garden, just one room above a cellar. A small shed in the garden served as an extra summer bedroom.

The studios themselves are simple: corrugated roofs, whitewashed stonework on the outside walls and white-framed glazing to the garden, rough concrete floors in the lower studio, terracotta tiles in the upper studio and the greenhouse. And yet, inhabited by Hepworth, these are captivating spaces, an affinity between the plaster casts and stone dust of her work and the soft limewash of

the walls, and the famously reflective St Ives light, filtered through the planting of the garden, giving clarity and precision to everything within, the whole having the focus of a space intended solely for work, and to consider that work.

The garden itself is quietly and cleverly designed to conceal the slope of the land and provide space for the display of over twenty sculptures, some very large. Being in the garden there is the sense of floating, belonging not to the streets around, but to the tower of the church alongside and the bay beyond. Taking these photographs, let in at dawn as an orange sun climbed free of the hills on the far bay to strike her sculptures and break into her buildings, we felt a greater connection with Hepworth even than walking among her work and standing in her studio where her coats hang as she left them: we were seeing the same sun she had seen.

It feels a place of belonging. It is hard to imagine Hepworth leaving it; she didn't like to. Can inert art long, a garden be a place of longing? Do we imbue places with meaning, or do they instil it in us? Many years after I first visited the garden, at Hepworth's Tate Britain retrospective, with her work crowded together in underground galleries without natural light, I was struck that the sculptures all seemed self-portraits, sharing her longing to return to the private, personal, protective world of her garden.

74   *The path to the greenhouse*

76   *Stone blocks awaiting carving*

77   *The outer stone wall from the street*

78–79   *Light falls on plaster maquettes and whitewashed walls in the carving studio*

80–81   *Sculptures and tree trunks occupying the garden*

82 *In the upper greenhouse*

83 *The church tower beyond the garden seen in morning light*

Silence

Silence

Possibly my favourite sound is the intense silence at the end of a perfect concert, just before the applause. Everything is heightened. At home, or when alone in the studio, I listen to music, almost instinctively, mostly Bach. There is noise. True silence is rare, but when it happens there is beauty in it. In silence you can truly listen to your thoughts, hear the movement of the air, your pen on a page.

Travel writer Patrick Leigh Fermor wrote his short book *A Time to Keep Silence* about arriving, unannounced, at a Benedictine monastery in northern France, seeking solace from a fast life in Paris, suffering writer's block and in need of a clear space, and of the change of pace, of time, of being, that the silence of his new surroundings would provide. Once he had passed the initial period of disquiet instilled by the silence of the monastery, he found that time had slowed, and that he began to notice small but slowly mutable things; the subtle intonements of plainsong, leaves changing on the trees, the shifting fall of light in his room.

> *The Abbey had emptied of guests and I had been shifted into an enormous cell. It was a wonderful room to wake up in. Sunlight streamed in through the three tall windows and, as I lay in bed, all I could see was layer on ascending layer of chestnut leaves ... and the crystalline sky of October framed by the thin reflected blue-white ... or, where the sun struck, white-gold surfaces of the walls and window-arches.*

And he began to write.

We need silence to know ourselves. Our spaces should provide this for us.

In his Pritzker Prize acceptance speech, Mexican architect Luis Barragán wrote that his spaces are not for those who shun silence, and I imagine mine are the same. I like to think that my spaces are ones in which you can be happily quiet; spaces in which you can read a book alone, have a quiet conversation. I'd like to think they encourage intimacy.

In silence all is heightened and you appreciate the details of a space; the texture of the walls, the meeting of materials, how light strikes a surface. It is hard not to find beauty in silence. Everything becomes important. I wonder if I conceive a building in its silent state. Spaces should allow for silence, though they can also be loud, and need to be considered in noise. A space should encourage conviviality, not echo unpleasantly.

I'd like my spaces to be ones that encourage the state Leigh Fermor finds in his monastery; if not always, then to allow for such moments of appreciation. The possibility of silence should be present.

To achieve silence, a space must feel solid, resolved. The proportions settled, views considered. Unnecessary detail removed, the palette of materials restrained. Nothing jarring. To be calm, rooms and spaces must flow logically, though they should also give surprise and delight. Light and shade held in balance, the space in conversation with nature. A sofa will be soft and comfortable. A table will not be noisy when you place something on it. The walls will not echo, cracks will not form.

If a window faces the wrong way, the right light will never fall on it. On Saturday evenings I like to lie in the bath listening to the opera on the radio, and so my bath faces west, to get the evening light. My mother always wanted a south-facing window in which to sit and embroider. She has just moved house at the age of eighty, and finally she has it.

There needs to be consideration for us as humans. There should be a generosity (if not of space then in other ways), a kindness. The walls should soothe. There should be a gentleness, which comes from having asked what is the best space for us, its user.

In the heightened state of silence, imperfections are laid bare. And so the implication is that a silent space must be perfect, everything considered. But of course no space can be perfect. The more you are forced to look, the closer you look, the more there are imperfections. That way lies madness. Buildings are not computer renderings. I like to use natural materials; their degrees of imperfectibility stop the eye looking for the perfect, allow it to come to rest. Spaces should accept imperfection, reveal the hand of their maker, their materiality, the marks of use and time.

Too much silence can be oppressive. Silence, visual silence, is not quiet. It is a place for our voices to be heard. And just as no silence is perfectly quiet, a space doesn't always need to be beautiful, but to possess the possibility of beauty.

Barragán also wrote that in the gardens he created, silence sings. I like the idea of silence singing. Just as silence sings, silent spaces should sing.

St James's Apartment

London UK 2018

This apartment in central London belongs to Japanese clients who come for short visits, which, added to their temperament, makes few demands on the space, allowing the project an unencumbered brief – essentially it simply needed to be a beautiful space for the days of the year when they are here.

Divided by two thick walls cutting cruciform through its centre, the apartment has a simple plan, and the building is protected, limiting the scope for change. The layout at the rear was slightly altered, and we reopened an original doorway between the two front rooms to open up the space and views through it: I like buildings where you can walk around in circles like this.

An archway was revealed in one of the crosswalls, inspiring the barrel-vaulted hall that now extends the full length of the apartment, ending in a semicircular sculpture niche, in which after much deliberation we left a sculptural Ingo Maurer folded paper lamp that happened to be placed there on delivery, accidentally perfect. A concealed panel halfway along the vault can be drawn across, closing the rear half to form an antechamber to the main bedroom beyond when privacy is wanted.

The vaulted hallway is finished in polished plaster. The space it contains has an incredible palpability: you can feel its form. The acoustic of the vault, as in the rest of the apartment, also plays a part. There is a sense of peace throughout.

Floors are in untreated English oak and a new fire surround was installed in Purbeck marble from Dorset, honed on the surround and flamed to the hearth.

On the first day of the works the entire contents of the former apartment were cleared out, and the project was an opportunity to select everything for a space anew – from the art on the walls and all the furniture to the Italian linen sheets, the cutlery (David Mellor Pride) and the crockery (David Mellor bone china). A wall hanging by artist-weaver Amy Revier was commissioned for the living room.

The wall lights that give rhythm to the hallway were designed for the space and cast in brass by the Carl Auböck Workshop in Vienna, so sharing their lineage with the five generations of elegant objects made there. The door pulls were similarly bespoke-designed and Auböck-crafted, inspired by handles from screens in the impossibly refined Katsura Imperial Villa outside Kyoto, the only direct nod to Japan in the apartment – except perhaps for the calm, refined atmosphere that its spaces maintain, removed from the busyness of Piccadilly Circus just a few steps away.

90   *A bespoke desk provides a place to write in the living room*

92–93   *Patterns of light in the living room*

94 & 95   *Framed views in the main bedroom*

Andrea Palladio

Villa Saraceno

Vicenza Italy 1550

Already the smallest of the villas depicted in Andrea Palladio's 1570 treatise *The Four Books of Architecture*, and smaller than it was drawn, with one of its intended side wings missing, the Villa Saraceno looks to be a modest building. If so it is a false modesty, as, experienced in person, the overwhelming impression is of its immense scale, although one so perfect in its proportion and generosity that it makes you wonder how you have lived in rooms of less than 6 metre (20 foot) ceiling height.

Perfectly offset against the grand scale is its utter simplicity. Reached up a generous set of steps, the vaulted entrance loggia leads in to one large room, the hall, and then straight out of a door at the rear, raised above the surrounding garden and fields beyond. This view straight through the villa gives a sense of openness, and also a diffidence, as if the space of the house, and the air within it, belongs not to the house but to the fields outside. It helps that the huge space of the hall is empty, its function simply to greet, and to give the pleasure of passing through.

On the left are the smarter rooms, a drawing room and smaller, vaulted study. In common with many of Palladio's villas, though again modest in comparison, these rooms are frescoed, but high up in an upper layer of the room, high enough to be out of sight so they don't visually intrude. Windows are tall, framed in timber with leaded lights of old glass and with pleasing metalwork

handles, the slight colour and thickness of the glass giving it a material presence. Otherwise there are terracotta-tiled floors, natural lime-rendered walls, simple timber plank doors and deep beamed ceilings. The external doors have no frame, but are held simply on iron hinges nailed into the stone surround. When open their framelessness reinforces the sense of open space.

To the right of the hall are a lower dining room and bedroom with huge fireplaces; another bedroom and bathrooms are on a mezzanine floor above them. An enclosed winding stone stair rises past the hall from the cellar below up to the attics above, low rooms of undulating brick floors where the grain harvest was stored, safe from intruders and rats.

The one lopsided wing, itself the size of a large country house, has the kitchen, a ping-pong room, more bedrooms and attics. The front half is given over to the *barchessa*, the open double-height loggia behind a giant order of Doric stone columns, so welcoming a space to sit that surely meals must have been enjoyed here since Biagio Saraceno built his villa nearly five centuries ago.

Despite the passage of so much time, the feeling being here is not of the immense age of the building, but instead of the immediacy of the space it so lightly contains, holding nothing more than the lightness of the northern Italian air as it passes silently through.

98   *Light falls into the loggia*

100–101   *Looking straight through the villa from the entrance gates, with the* barchessa *wing to the side. Palladio intended a matching wing to the left*

102–103   *The empty purity of the hall under its 6 metre (20 foot) high ceiling, its door openings framed in plain stone*

104 *Purity in a side wing bedroom under the roof*

105 *The undulating brick floor of the attic granary, a secure grain store lying directly over the drawing room and study*

106–107 *Light and shade in the barchessa, an outdoor room*

108   *Rough-plastered walls, stone-flagged floor and ping-pong in the side wing*

109   *A brick wall and double screen of lime trees frame the garden to the front of the villa*

Peter Zumthor

Secular Retreat

Devon UK 2018

The Secular Retreat was built as part of Living Architecture's series of houses intended to provide the experience of contemporary architecture to anyone – like a modern Landmark Trust, custodians of the preceding Villa Saraceno – and in this it is revelatory, transformative, so far do its spaces transcend the experience of an ordinary home.

Its Swiss architect, Peter Zumthor, likens it to a Palladian villa, like the Saraceno, for the command of the landscape it surveys, but to my reading it is less classical and more Neolithic, like a mystic henge of unknown origin, massive piers holding up the heavy roof like ancient stones, or like elders holding aloft shelter for villagers to congregate under. The bedrooms, too, have the ancient permanence of caves carved out of rock, spaces of retreat from which to look out, protected by the ring of Monterey pines that were planted presumably as a windbreak around the house that formerly occupied the site, so ordinary as if in wilful denial of its beauty, and which now give the place the feeling of a tumulus.

The Retreat provides a huge living room – hall, cooking, eating, seating around a fire, and study in one space – with five bedrooms in two irregularly angled blocks leading off as if monoliths knocked over by a passing giant. In the absence of walls, with windows, the extraordinary becomes ordinary. Instead of walls there is 5 metre (16 foot) high triple glazing, whose opening panes seal shut the

110   *The house in its ring of protective Monterey pines*

howling winds outside with the satisfaction of a Swiss train door. The bedrooms are reached along a glazed corridor raised above the ground outside so that it feels as if you float to bed as a ghost. The living room inspires conviviality, but it also provides spaces at its edges to sit apart and silently contemplate the forces that created the folding valleys below.

To pour concrete is to build twice: first the formwork built in reverse and then the concrete itself poured within; and the roof, both massive and apparently floating, is in fact constructed in two pours, one internal and one external, concealing a layer of insulation within.

All is faultlessly executed. Wardrobes in applewood fit perfectly into reveals cast in the concrete, despite it being built up in layers poured a day at a time, like an archaeological section. The cherrywood bedroom floors stop just short of the walls without the modesty of a skirting board to hide their edge. The irregular layout of the Blue Lias stone floor is set out and cut with a perfection that to the masons of cathedrals would once have been second nature, but now requires concerted exactitude from all.

The house has an effortless ease, but is a building of incredible dedication and commitment, and of such rarity that it somehow places us not just in our recent past but in the millennia of time, and gives a wholly new perspective on the relationship between the Earth and our place on it.

112   *The massive roof slab floating over walls of glass*

114–115   *The folds of the valleys take on new significance surveyed from the house*

116–117   *Massive concrete columns inside and out in conversation with the pine trees*

118   *Layers of concrete form the living room fireplace block*

119   *A corner for reading and writing*

120   *The pattern of floor slabs echoes the interplay of the roof slabs above*

121   *The bedroom corridor: 'like floating to bed as a ghost'*

122   *Joinery sits perfectly within apertures in the concrete walls*

123   *Bathing becomes a ritual to be marked*

Mountain Chateau

Haute-Savoie France 2019

I recall walking up into the attic of this seventeenth-century chateau deep in the French Alps for the first time, and the sense of delighted awe at coming up the corner stair into the cathedral-like space, the particular smell and atmosphere of dry timber, and the indirect daylight glowing up from the open eaves around the perimeter.

The original three-hundred-and-fifty-year-old structure was painstakingly analysed but found to be beyond repair, and apart from the two massive rough-rendered chimney stacks coming up through the space, all was removed and a new structure constructed by local master carpenter Bertrand Pegorier, its frame erected by two mountain climbers and a giant crane.

The clients had assumed the converted space would be plastered, but to me it seemed obvious that it should be timber, now perhaps the strongest impression of the space. The roof is lined in brushed French larch boards, with oak boards on the floor. River-washed pebbles form a hearth around the suspended fireplace, and the chimneys were hand rendered with rough local lime render.

Shafts of light coming in through the three storeys of dormer windows and rooflights reveal the scale of the space. The perimeter is uplit, recalling the reflected daylight that once entered through the open eaves, interrupted only where the attic meets an older medieval tower, now

124   *The chateau sits on the outskirts of a village at the end of a valley deep in the French Alps; the backdrop is framed by mountains*

housing a discrete shower room, and meaning that the space of the attic always remains legible despite its size.

To keep the perimeter of the space clear, two uplit timber stacks, recalling the local way of drying timber, house a small kitchen, and a store of boards and mattresses that can be brought out to form table tops on trestles, or bed bases to be wheeled around, with lights plugged into sockets in the floor.

The original sensations have been recreated in the reconstructed space, and whether used as impromptu concert hall, badminton court in winter when the grounds are hidden in snow, overspill party dormitory or cinema, there is always the sense of the space as a retreat, quietly apart from the domestic spaces of the house below, still evoking the awestruck feeling of the original attic.

126   *The vaulted stairwell rises through the chateau leading to the attic*

128–129   *The three-storey-high reconstructed attic. Lighting around the perimeter recalls the formerly open eaves*

130   *Light falling through the space reveals its scale*

131   *The original roof was in a poor state, and removed in its entirety. The two chimney stacks were the only structures retained*

132   *Mattress bases can be wheeled out to form beds*

133   *A projector screen lowers down from behind a beam*

Shadows

Shadows

We are afraid of shadows. Understandably. Architects no less than others: buildings are invariably photographed in full sun; architectural writing talks of light, shadows rarely mentioned. And yet when we make a building we make shadows, not light.

Shadows reveal form, allow us to read texture. They provide nuance and reveal beauty.

Japanese writer Jun'ichirō Tanizaki wrote his beautiful book *In Praise of Shadows* about how, in building a house for himself, through the focused gaze the process entailed he became aware of a Japanese sensibility, and developed an appreciation of shadow and its embrace.

> *And so it has come to be that the beauty of a Japanese room depends on a variation of shadows; heavy shadows against light shadows – there is nothing else.*

To go to Japan is to be witness to a refined sensibility. I am English, and like Japan, England is a nuanced place, secluded, shaded, distinctions made in degrees of subtlety.

Though, I am writing this on a Greek island, where I have sought the shade, away from the heat and light. Here the most special, sacred spaces, the chapels across the alley opposite and in the monastery up the hill, are the places of greatest darkness. They require you to stay, to linger, for your eyes to adjust to them. In doing so you form a relationship with the building, in time as well as space. Your emotions are engaged, an intimacy develops.

Back home in England the light is less intense, windows are bigger, shadows more nuanced, their edges softer. When building in our muted climate, we tend to want to extract and savour what light we get, and so forget shadow, and our need for shelter.

I have an etching by Henry Moore, a small dark square, atypically not of a figure but of an architectural doorway revealed in indirect side light. Etching starts with a dark plate, and then the process of etching, each etched mark, brings light in, revealing and describing space. Swiss architect Peter Zumthor ^{PP. 110–123} writes of conceiving a space in darkness, then of letting light into it.

Perhaps we should think of, conceive of, our spaces in candlelight. This warm, changing light suits our human frailty, the flickering light falling on our walls as on Tanizaki's shadowed lacquerware.

Shadows are rarely black. Shadows vary through the day and through the year, become more prevalent, longer, more or less intense. Shadow's medium is subtlety. The photographs here were shot on film, revealing a complexity and depth within the shadows, much closer to how we experience the world ourselves. Is this why they seem to capture the soul of the spaces?

A few years ago, I had a sudden desire to learn to paint in oils, which I had never done, and took a week off to go on a course. We were instructed to paint some wooden cubes on a table, paying particular attention to the shade of light on each plane, grading the tone from one to five. I found I was more interested in the penumbra of each object, the glow where its shadow met the light, and concentrated on painting this. Interestingly, my fellow students painted very precise cubes, as you would expect an architect to, while mine were hazy. The teacher claimed not to be able to see what I was painting, denied the existence of the penumbra. She may just have been annoyed at my failure to follow her instructions. I wonder if perhaps we wish to inhabit the penumbra, the space between.

A room cannot be all glass. Of Mies van der Rohe's Farnsworth House, a house that attempted to banish shadows, the owner, Edith Farnsworth, wrote that in the house she felt 'always on the alert, always restless'. As much as buildings celebrate light, as much as we delight in the falling of light on them, we also need shelter and comfort. There are times we need to look inwards, to retreat, to find the place that is like closing your eyes to become invisible as a child. We need quiet, and shadows are quiet places. They provide comfort. My spaces are layered, they make space for our humanity. I hope they have a tenderness.

The most intense music concert I ever experienced was pianist Grigory Sokolov, a small stooped figure of intense energy, playing in black tails and in almost complete darkness, just one lamp on the keyboard. The darkness intensified the music and the space. Perhaps it was this that enabled him to play also with time: old pieces felt new, contemporary pieces timeless, just as I see architecture, outside of time, existing only now, through the seasons, in memory.

Architecture exists in space and light, but it also belongs in time, and shadows reveal this, ephemeral, never the same. However open they may be, at the end of every day all buildings go into shade, and darkness.

Geoffrey Bawa

Lunuganga

Bentota Sri Lanka 1948–1988

Lunuganga, 'Salt River', was the country house of Sri Lankan architect Geoffrey Bawa, an old plantation bungalow sited on 25 acres (10 hectares) across a spit into the Dedduwa Lake in the southwest of the country. It is a climate where gardening is by cutting back rather than planting, and a place where you are conscious of shadows, whether of sun or rain.

It is said that Bawa designed buildings as he would gardens, and that when making gardens he sought to create atmospheres. He lived at Lunuganga for over fifty years, and as his career developed it became his retreat, a place of experimentation, expansive in counterpoint to the containment of his townhouse in Colombo.[pp. 166–177]

The house is full of beautiful things but its spaces are comfortable rather than radical. Bawa had a sunken outdoor bath in a courtyard off his bedroom, open to the sky. The house was reordered; the former entrance became the main garden terrace, the garage a covered terrace, the main living room opening on to it. Time here is mostly spent outdoors.

Bawa had swathes cut through the jungle to reveal views out to the surrounding lake; a hill crest on the front side of the garden was lowered so that he could see the shimmer of the lake from his breakfast table.

[138] *The baroque terrace edge to the upper lawn, an Italian reference*

A frangipani tree on the terrace, in fact two grafted together, is the fulcrum around which the whole garden pivots, to which your sense of space wherever you are is tied. Its boughs were weighed down so that they spread out over the terrace; as much as the tree itself you are aware of its etiolated shadows playing on the lawn. Beyond, a baroque brick curlicue forms the terrace edge. To be up here, raised above the water below, among the birds, is as if you are a god.

Leading down and below, a series of paths descends in the shade of the high terrace walls, never dictating but always offering a choice of route, an act of kindness, so that you become part of Bawa's creation as you make your way through it.

Through the garden, framing terrace edges, Bawa built a series of pavilions – a gate lodge bridging the ha-ha, a guest room with glazed walls suspended over the entrance courtyard, his private art gallery stepping down the hill – each an architectural experiment, and now a hotel room.

The garden provides darkness, shade and revelation, places to stop. Movement and shade correlate; you become a participant in the garden, or part of the shadows. There is a sense always of floating. To be in the garden is otherworldly, and life-affirming.

140   *Seating in the outdoor living room*

142–143   *Paving extends the grid of the house to the outside, set against the meandering shadows of the frangipani tree*

144–145   *The outdoor living room was formerly the house's garage*

146 & 147   *The simple lines of the Bishop's Passage, leading into the house from the front door*

148–149   *The Glass House, raised to avoid an immense tree, both frames and gives shade to the entrance court*

150–151   *Sculptures poised over the lake below. Bawa didn't like perfection, and had the arms removed*

London Woodland

London UK 2014

This project created, from a series of quintessentially English rooms – drawing room, dining room and study, breakfast room, kitchen and pantry – a flow of generous connected living spaces.

The plan fell naturally into place without complication. Others would probably have glazed in the open loggia overlooking the garden, but cutting down its wisteria would have felt like sacrilege, and it provides dappled shade to the south-facing garden elevation. Instead the dining room was extended sideways, with a glazed extension cantilevered over a new walled orchard garden that it overlooks to the side.

Not long after the house was built, its main drawing room, now the living room, had been extended into the garden, leaving its fireplace awkwardly off-centre; it was unified in the space by placing it within an extended fire surround above a hearth that extends the length of the room, all in slabs of flamed Purbeck marble from the south coast of England. The library, living and dining spaces use the original house's slightly irregular, pinwheel plan to provide variety of outlook and use, enigmatically hovering between being a single open space and discernible rooms.

The kitchen is separated from the main living spaces, at the client's wish, running along the side of the house, with a 10 metre (33 foot) long stainless steel worktop connecting the front of the house to the back. The slabs of its sandstone floor align with the run of kitchen cupboards.

152   *The house's original hallway was reconfigured with wide floorboards and tall double pivot doors leading to the living room*

There is a pervading calm. The whole interior is painted a single shade of shaded white. The main ground floor living spaces have a magical warmth, from the southern garden light falling on new English oak floorboards. Upstairs, soft grey wool carpets give a welcome coolness to a generous series of bedrooms, with polished plaster bathrooms. Throughout, elements of oak joinery give warmth. The client collected beautiful and comfortable furniture and art for the house.

Photographed several years on from completion, the client's pottery collection, including her own work thrown in a pottery created from the old garage, populates the house happily in the shadows of the warm light.

The large garden, formerly an English gentleman's dream of manicured lawn with nervous flowerbeds stuck around its edges, was taken up and English woodland trees were planted as if an extension of the nearby common, screening its boundaries, laid out to create two lawned clearings within.

There is a generous friendliness to the house: I think this comes from the south light, and the spaces just open and large enough that you can be in your own private space but in calling distance of others. Within the frame of an older house have been created wonderful spaces to be in. Periodically I receive messages from the owner simply saying, I love this house.

154   *I'm not sure where the inspiration came from for the brass door detail. Perhaps because of this it gives me great satisfaction*

156–157   *Looking from the shaded library into the main living room; spaces connected but distinct*

158   *Dappled light falling into the dining room, with the living room beyond*

159   *The living room fireplace hearth runs the length of the room*

160–161   *The end of the dining room was extended, with a glazed end wall and cantilevered structure to float over the walled side garden*

162   *The 10 metre (33 foot) long stainless steel worktop was fabricated in one piece, and runs the length of the kitchen*

163   *The original wisteria-covered loggia beyond was retained, to shade and filter the south light coming in from the garden*

164–165   *Long linen curtains fall on the soft grey carpet of the main bedroom*

Geoffrey Bawa

Number 11

Colombo Sri Lanka 1960–1998

Bawa's town house in Colombo, the other side of his psyche and counterpart to his expansive country house, Lunuganga,[pp. 138–151] was formed during the same fifty-year period, and similarly was a place of experimentation, here within the containment of a residential urban block.

It started as a series of four low row-houses that Bawa slowly acquired and expanded into, accessed along a side passage that now forms the entrance hall to the combined house. The ground floor is entirely inward-looking, based around small contemplative courtyards, which the tropical climate allows to be open and which trees now outgrow, some with water trickling, the sound taking the mind away from the urban world outside.

Passing the 1930s Rolls-Royce in which Bawa would drive to Lunuganga, down two steps, the long hall internalizes and deflects, ending in a courtyard pool, the entrance to the house proper never entirely explicit. To the side is the central but private living room, with a dining room, a study and Bawa's bedroom suite leading off, rooms of spatial variation, the central ones tall under raised ceilings, those to the side with roofs lowering around reflecting pools that bring the sky into the space, and all populated by Bawa's eclectic collection of possessions and artworks. Each space leads into another or out to an enclosed courtyard, so that to be inside or out becomes indistinguishable. Floors inside are painted white, adding to a sense of abstraction.

166   *The white-painted floor of the entrance corridor, once an external alleyway that led to four separate houses*

Back at the front of the house a tight stair leads up to the 10 metre (33 foot) long sitting room over the entrance garage, indirectly lit from a raised light box at one end, its blank wall to the street covered with a Balinese wall hanging. With its white-painted floor and shag pile rugs, and Bawa's assemblage of antique and twentieth-century furniture in timber and plastic, it is possibly the coolest room I have ever been in.

The stair continues up to a covered roof terrace that once looked out, like Lunuganga, to water, here to the sea; that view is now blocked, which stresses today the private interior world the house creates.

In this house all is indirect. Movement is never in a straight line, but rather winds, through confined and unexpected spaces, giving delight and a sense of discovery. Views are framed and contained. Light enters the house mostly through small courtyards, so that the role of the house is to provide shade, and the experience of the house is like that of the light entering it: reflected, controlled and offset against shadow.

168 *Looking back along the entrance corridor, with the Rolls-Royce housed in the garage at the far end*

170–171 *Timber ceiling mirrors terracotta floor tiles in the dining room*

172–173 *Rooms open out into contained courtyards, which the trees try to escape*

176   *The roof terrace, from where there were once views over Colombo to the sea*

177   *The fretwork entrance and garage doors on to the street*

New York Apartment

New York City USA 2020

On the first site trip out to New York I found myself wondering how creating a space there would differ from creating one in London; what the nuances of the respective cities mean for their spaces. And so, on arriving, I was thrown to discover that the apartment, in fairly original condition in a 1910 building on Manhattan's Upper West Side, had a distinctly Scandinavian feeling, with its open white-panelled spaces and original parquet floors. I was transported to Copenhagen or Stockholm rather than New York.

The landmark status of the apartment building meant that no changes were permitted to the exterior. Apartment blocks already impose tight constraints, but the decision was taken on that first trip to retain the coffered ceilings, misaligned to the windows below and the panelling below that, and to keep the original parquet floors, a rare survival, so eliminating any notions of radical intervention.

The apartment was instead subverted more subtly. The resulting space is a nuanced place, flowing in degrees of informality, in varied and numerous ways.

The apartment is raised a floor above the street, and its living rooms, from den to library, dining room, reading room and living room, follow the street outside as if walking around the apartment is to walk the sidewalk, but without the traffic. Flowing through and behind this is the fluid interior

of the apartment; degrees of shaded, protective space. It is never a series of formal rooms, but rather a series of connected spaces, the layers of space marked by bespoke blackened steel shelving, allowing connections to be permeable, for that permeability to be varied. The glazed wall in the kitchen connects the inner courtyard to the leaves of the street outside.

The space of the apartment is complex, as it should be: perhaps it is an English sensibility, but I think that the space of an apartment, arranged on one floor and sandwiched between notionally identical spaces above and below, must make itself distinct, must express the spirit of its inhabitants, transcend its proximities and provide the sense of separation, of going to bed, that a house can give. The open flowing space needed shadow.

An Ellsworth Kelly sculpture at MoMA inspired the sapele cladding that marks introspective transitional moments throughout that provide this sense: the entrance vestibule, reveals off the hall, the lobby that separates the bedrooms and conceals the service spaces in the centre of the apartment, providing moments of shade within the open flowing space that runs through the apartment. Having opened up the apartment and removed shadow, we brought it back in.

In the end, the space of New York flows through the apartment so that within it, it could be nowhere else.

180   *A corner of the reading room. The apartment has its original parquet flooring*

182–183   *The wraparound living rooms. Bespoke shelving layers the space*

184   *A leather-lined wall in the entrance hall*

185   *Shelving frames a dining space at the entrance to the apartment*

186   *An inner glazed wall allows views from the kitchen through the apartment*

187   *The breakfast table in a window seat overlooking the courtyard of the block*

188   *A vaulted ceiling finished in polished plaster over the master shower*

189   *Sapele cladding lines the bedroom corridor*

Life

Life

For all that we consider our spaces, put care into them, they must not be sterile or made for photographs, but created for us: they must be alive, be spaces for lives to be lived in. Designing spaces must come from an understanding of our sensitivities and humanity, of care for it.

Our spaces should follow, not dictate, our lives. This happens surprisingly rarely, but then it is hard to really know how we live, and how we might live and work, to interrogate and acknowledge what is important in the ritual of our daily lives. The architect's role is to tease this out, to intuit it, and then to give the ritual and life form.

Jim Ede asked this. In his book *A Way of Life* he distils the life essence that runs through Kettle's Yard, the house–gallery he created with his wife, Helen, in 1950s Cambridge.[PP 206–217] Objects of everyday life are treated with the same reverence as art – which also means that art is treated as everyday. This attitude, the relationship it fosters between objects and between object and user, and the space it created, was – and remains – quietly revolutionary.

Kettle's Yard is filled with, only contains, objects that had care put into their making. This seems true even of the circular pebbles the Edes collected on Norfolk beaches. We sense the care that goes into making something, and when we use it we pass that care into the world. This is the same with spaces. The huge effort involved – from client, to architect and builder – in making a truly good space passes on to its users, its inhabitants. If a space is alive it makes us feel alive. And it works the other way round, too – we give spaces life by inhabiting them, and we should not feel scared of the expression of that life on the space.

We seek beautiful, perfect interiors, and then life messes them up. It brings in favoured objects, places washing up in our sinks, dogs on our sofas, people in the way of art on the walls. This is inevitable, and we must find beauty in its imperfection.

To describe the feeling a new house might have I am fond of saying to clients that they should be able to drag a log basket across it without ruining the floor. This sometimes gets strange looks from them, who perhaps have come in search of perfection. But a space must be robust, be able to accept scuffs and kicks and not to mind; in fact, to get better. For this the architecture cannot be surface deep. Not to look its best the day it is finished, but instead to age gracefully, to revel in the marks of time, to withstand and accept them, and get richer for them.

The best architecture is enhanced by good objects of any period placed in it; the same holds true for good art or music in the space. A space should be able to take a hard-edged but beautiful chair, or a favourite old kilim rug. I find spaces filled with only old things perturbing: where is the life force? And similarly with only new things: where is your past?

A space to view art can have life and an attitude, does not need to retreat to invisibility. I long to design a gallery with rough limewashed walls that simply get patched over after each rehang, for a patina to develop.

If art makes us scared we may not wish to live with it. Similarly, we should not be scared of our spaces, be in awe of them. Instead they should liberate us, we should feel free within them, at home. Life should course through them. We should allow beautiful things in, in conversation with one another and with the space. Good spaces stimulate us, invigorate us.

Describing the spaces here, I find the words I wish to use are the same as I would want to use of a friend: warm, grounded, kind, gentle, thoughtful, exciting. Buildings are like people: you want to spend time with them as you would a friend.

Spending time in these buildings and gardens, photographing them, what comes across most is the life that is in them, the life force that made them: the simple desire to create something beautiful.

Bloomsbury Apartment

London UK 2010

I realize I have lived in this flat now for over fifteen years, a twentieth of its three-hundred-year life. Before an old friend and I took it on as my home and his office, it had been an office of bland indifference to the history of the building and the sense of delight it gives every morning as the sun shines down the street opposite into the front rooms, and each afternoon as dappled light falls through the planting on the terrace at the rear.

The spaces have witnessed the same light since the house was built three centuries ago, when the end of this densely planned urban street was the edge of London, with fields beyond. As London's gravity moved west, the street became less smart, and the ground floor became a shop. The crooked stairs have been on a slow decline throughout.

The traces of the office were removed, stone flags laid in the hall, the fireplaces opened up and floorboards revealed, scrubbed bare, the panelling painted mattest white, the bathroom silver, an abundantly planted terrace added at the rear, but otherwise the spaces are as they always have been, and you fit in with them, although much is not as old as it might seem: a false floor put in upstairs, presumably to protect the plaster ceilings below, means that the rooms are raised two steps, and all the panelling dates from then. I realized it is this that makes the windows slightly oversized, the sills lower than expected, and gives the upstairs rooms their particular sense of floating.

Deep cupboards either side of the fireplace upstairs hide books, CDs and the stereo, and a wardrobe in the bedroom my clothes, and meant I could move in with just a chair, a bed and a chest of drawers. Things have been creeping in slowly ever since.

It took four years to find a sofa with the right balance of line and comfort to collapse on to at the end of each day, longer to find a piano, voiced by plucking the felt of its hammers to soften the sound for the space (and neighbours). And one by one have come rugs, chairs for guests to sit on and lights for them to read by; ceramics have collected on the piano. The panelling is dictatorial when it comes to picture hanging, and pictures stay happily on the floor, seated among the people in the room, occasionally moving around, or on, their presence felt much like guests in the room.

The most recent arrival is the armature holding the *fórcola*, the sculptural antique oarlock of a Venetian gondola, fabricated by Carlo Scarpa's metalworkers in their workshop in Venice among pieces of his buildings now being repaired, itself several years in the designing and making.

Each new arrival shifts the equilibrium of the room, requiring the next piece to swing it back, on a never-ending search for a peaceful balance. I think this needs time, though ideally there would be more rooms, and less stuff. A palazzo awaits.

196   *A vintage fórcola, the oarlock of a Venetian gondola, is held in an armature made by Carlo Scarpa's metalworkers in Venice*

198–199   *Light pours into the living room; furniture and objects find their place*

200 *Pictures rest on the floor as if guests in the room*

201 *A pelargonium reaches for light*

Sir Leslie Martin

Kettle's Yard

Cambridge UK 1957 & 1970

Jim Ede must have been a gentle person; his wife Helen too. As a Tate curator in the 1920s and 1930s, Ede assisted and supported artists – and in so doing amassed a superlative collection of works from the period.

He wrote beautifully on making a place by simply whitewashing its walls and placing a rug on scrubbed floors, and it feels as if this is all he did at Kettle's Yard. Returning from Tangiers in the 1950s, wanting to house his collection, Ede fancied laying down his rugs in a crumbling stately home in the countryside outside Cambridge. Instead he was offered four abandoned workers' cottages just outside the centre, knocked together with the economy of good design. There is a subtle sophistication in the way, for example, the walls curve up to meet the ceilings, softening and dissolving their space. Bay windows on the ground floor add light and space to the tightly defined spaces. After the narrow winding stair the long first floor room manages to come as a surprise.

An extension was added by Leslie Martin in 1970, after Kettle's Yard was formally given to Cambridge University. It is hard now to imagine the house without its extension beyond. Reached through the original house and a crank in the plan, the narrower width of the extension's upper floor continues the house's domestic scale and linearity. Below, disguising its almost square plan, it is divided church-like into a double-height central nave and lower toplit side aisles. The extension is experienced internally, an introspective space without external form. The brick floor, which feels

The ground floor spaces of the original cottages: everything in repose

so much a part of Kettle's Yard's identity, in fact belongs to the extension only, taken from the old house's fire hearths. It is a place for music: there is a second grand piano. Jacqueline du Pré played at the opening.

A place of its contents as much as their container, Kettle's Yard was conceived foremost as a place for conversations to happen: verbal, with the students Ede encouraged to visit; and visual, both between the viewer and objects, and between the objects themselves.

Objects are lit from the side and from above, set against a backdrop of rough whitewashed plaster. Artworks sit alongside objects, which sit alongside visitors. A collection of particularly spherical pebbles arranged in a diminishing circle, disparate armchairs covered in loose white covers, a Georgian glass on a fireplace, a modestly framed Ben Nicholson painted relief – all are placed with equal precision and delicacy in a conversation of equals. Sculptures rest happily on old tables or chests of drawers, pictures are placed low, to be contemplated by seated viewers. Every object gets the chance to sit and capture light.

It is this sense of equality, of all being alike, a sense of honesty under the same even gaze, I think, that gives Kettle's Yard its air of peace. It could feel daunting to live up to such perfection, but instead its gentleness feels soothing, like no other place.

208 *Works by Ben Nicholson and Alfred Wallace in Jim Ede's bedroom*

210   *Constantin Brancusi's cast-cement head* Prometheus *from 1912 rests on the piano*

211   *The Bechstein room, named after the piano, from the top of the stairs; a space for music and reading*

212   *The space at the top of the steps is a short bridge over an alleyway passing underneath, to connect the cottages at first floor level*

213   *Henri Gaudier-Brzeska's Dancer from 1913 dances in the sun*

214–215   *Peace finds a home in a corner of the extension*

216–217   *Objects in conversation sit on the brick floor in the double-height extension*

Stephen Marshall

Roche Court

Wiltshire UK 1998 & 2001

For what seem pleasant years but I realize stretch nearly to decades, I have been visiting and encouraging country-going friends to visit Roche Court in Wiltshire, home of gallerist Madeleine Bessborough.

With the lease on her London gallery up in 1994, the New Art Centre moved to the country, so starting a new way of showing art – outside – and genre of gallery.

Initially art was shown out in the gardens and park of the house, then also in the Gallery and later in the Artists House, allowing progressively smaller and more domestic works to be shown.

Roche Court, its landscape, buildings and art, is a magical place, sitting quietly in its hidden valley. The magic nestles where modern art meets classic English country house, showing how the one can be tamed and the other given life.

Madeleine tells the tale of the history of the Gallery building, writing to the big architectural names of the day with her grand ambition and less grand budget, and ultimately finding Stephen Marshall in a magazine article read at the hairdresser's. I remember reading about the Gallery in *The Architectural Review* when I was finishing at Edinburgh. Coming south, nothing was lost in seeing it; the glazed link stretching between house and orangery remained pretty much the

perfect architectural response; so perfect that it is now impossible to imagine Roche Court without it.

And I was bound to like the Artists House that followed, based as it is on Kettle's Yard, [pp. 206–217] and through Madeleine's lens the best interpretation of the original I can think of, probably because it primarily actually is a house for art and only passingly for living in. It manages to offer the same sense of the perfect response as the Gallery, but to a much more complicated brief and in a more complex context, tucked into what was a gap in the stable courtyard just behind the house.

Out in the park Antony Gormley figures stared at each other across the bluebell wood before ever they stared across London roofs; a Richard Long line of flints (*Tame Buzzard Line*, 2001) gives life to a dead tree and to his transient art. Madeleine's late husband Arthur's contribution to the scene was the herd of Jersey cows that tread beyond, looking for all the world (and perhaps to anyone buying) like a fellow art installation, the exact colour of a rusted Gormley figure or Anthony Caro arch.

It is hard to conceive of perfection, but it would probably be this sense of the permanent and the new. Finding the house still sitting at the end of its hidden drive, severe in Chilmark stone yet gentle under broad eaves and surrounded by art, has the same unexpected feeling each time, as if were you to come again it would be gone, making you savour it the more.

220   *Art placed in conversation with nature*

222–223   *It is hard to imagine the Gallery not being there, so well does it sit between the house and the orangery*

224–225   *The Gallery as vitrine. The exhibition is Edmund de Waal's 2020 show* tacet

Lewes Rectory

East Sussex UK 2013

A brick rectory built in 1911, and first sold, unaltered, to our client the potter Olivia Horley and her family a hundred years later in 2011. The original house was content with expressing solid dependability rather than elegance, and, seemingly designed for another site, the roof at the back of the house sloped down low, only for the garden to slope straight back up, too steep to use. The sunny front garden had been tarmacked over.

The first time I went to see the house, Olivia remembers me walking upstairs, turning towards the rear garden and saying that she should be able to go straight out into the garden from there. And so you can: we took the sloping roof at the back off, and brought a flat roof under a lawn, large enough to play games on. The landing now leads out on to it. We also added a potting studio under the garden for Olivia, lit by a skylight set flush into the lawn above.

Between these and the main rooms at the front of the house, the old kitchen, scullery and the rector's breakfast room were knocked into one linear cooking and dining space, entirely glazed at each end on to courtyards paved in local black bricks, receiving morning and evening light. The outside runs through this space so that here the house turns itself inside out. The new spaces have concrete floors that belong more to Olivia's studio than to an old rectory.

It would have been prohibitive to double glaze the original windows – a complicated arrangement of sash windows means there are sixty panes on the front elevation alone – so instead a wood-burning stove was installed in the central stair hall, sitting on a thermally massive concrete plinth, to soak up and radiate heat around the house.

The main rooms at the front were fine, and were left untouched, though the timber of the original parquet floors, the staircase and the doors was stripped bare, giving a material unity. No attempt was made to alter the rooms to follow the remodelled spaces being created behind; instead the two are allowed to exist in tandem.

Does this duality make the remodelled house a work of radical intervention, or of restrained economy? Perhaps it is both. Looking back, there is a shared robustness to both the new and the old spaces; and there is also a similar free-flowing airiness running through the front rooms and into the stair hall and landing as through the glass-ended space of the new kitchen. Along with Olivia's carefully chosen objects and art that run through the house, rather than anything tangible in the architecture, it is this abstract shared feeling that ties the house together.

234   *The kitchen was created from three back service rooms knocked together*

236–237   *Each end of the kitchen is completely glazed*

238　　*Local black bricks pave the outside courtyards*

239　　*Soft tones of cupboards, hand-made Delft tiles and the patina of the concrete floor*

240 *A wood-burning stove placed on a concrete plinth sends heat into the stair hall and landing above*

241 *Olivia's pottery collection bravely placed on shelves in the playroom*

242   *Sculptures rest in the stair window*

243   *Olivia's pottery studio. The calm focus of a place of making*

Directory of Plans

From a young age I have been fascinated by architectural plans. In the days before estate agents' details gave them, I would piece together houses' plans from the description and photographs, and then sort them out, fix what seemed to be their deficiencies.

Architectural plans are a slice taken at about table height through each floor of a building, a brutal act if enacted, to be viewed god-like from above. To some they are never more than an indecipherable pattern of lines, to others they reveal a building. To me they answer questions about how its spaces connect, a puzzle completed, and it pleases me to have them.

The plans of the buildings on these pages are shown at the same scale, 1:325. They reveal a huge variety in their actual scales and forms, but also, to me, a shared repose.

London UK
2020
330m² 3,550 sq ft

London Modernism

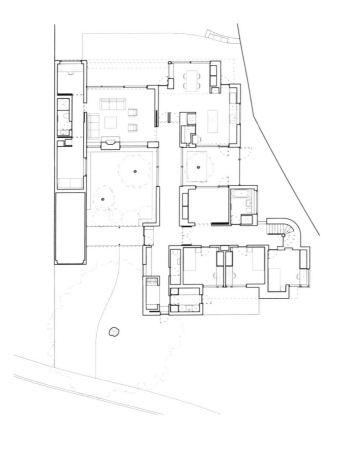

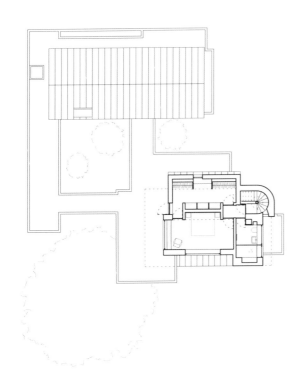

Luis Barragán
Mexico City   Mexico
1948–1988
817m²   8,800 sq ft

Casa Barragán

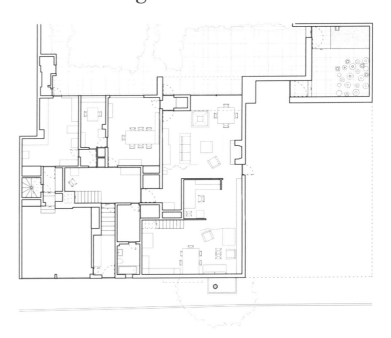

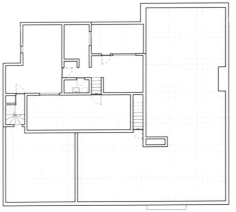

with James Gorst Architects
Oxfordshire UK
2011 & 2014
820m² 8,825 sq ft

London UK
2018
100m² 1,075 sq ft

Oxfordshire Farm

St James's Apartment

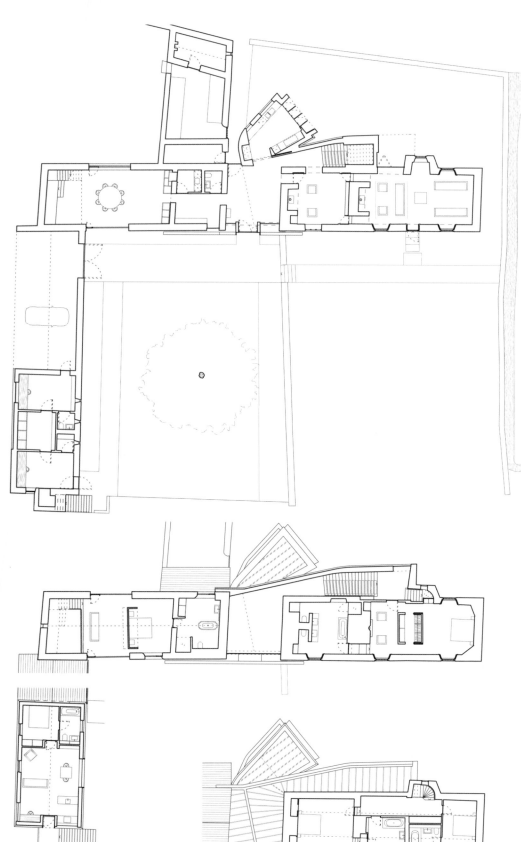

Andrea Palladio
Vicenza Italy
1550
1,436m²   15,460 sq ft

Villa Saraceno

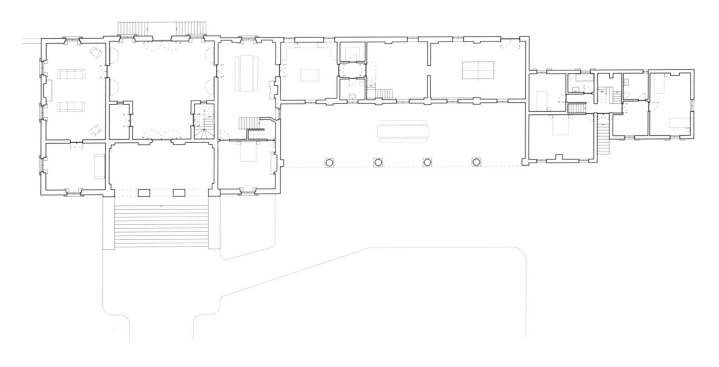

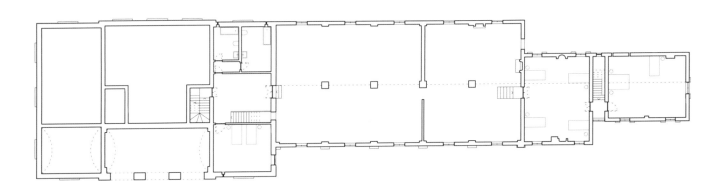

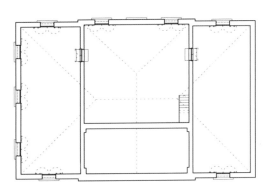

Peter Zumthor
Devon   UK
2018
375m²   4,040 sq ft

Secular Retreat

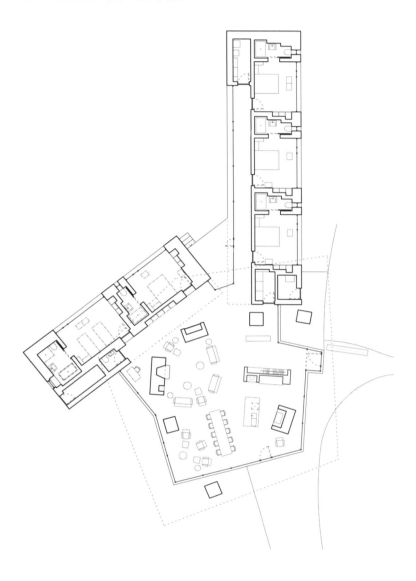

Haute-Savoie   France
2019
270m²   2,900 sq ft

Mountain Chateau

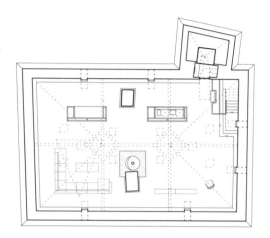

London   UK
2014
550m²   5,920 sq ft

Geoffrey Bawa
Colombo   Sri Lanka
1960–1998
560m²   6,030 sq ft

New York City   USA
2020
300m²   3,230 sq ft
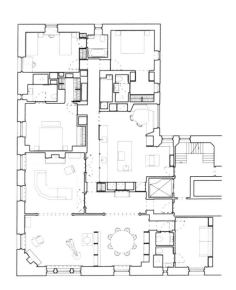

London Woodland

Number 11

New York Apartment

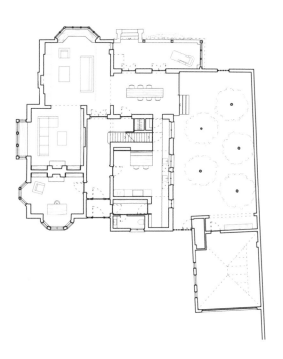

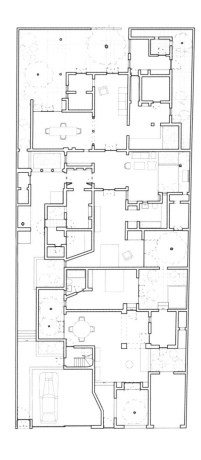

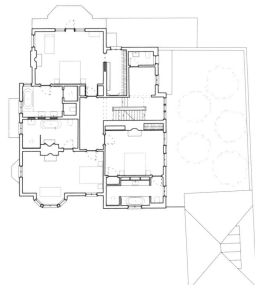

London   UK
2010
155m²   1,670 sq ft

Sir Leslie Martin
Cambridge   UK
1957 & 1970
760m²   8,180 sq ft

Bloomsbury Apartment   Kettle's Yard

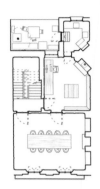

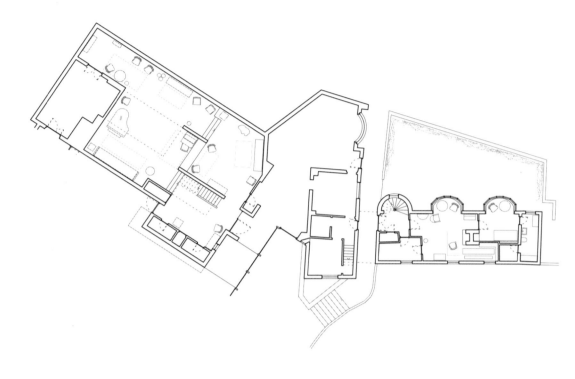

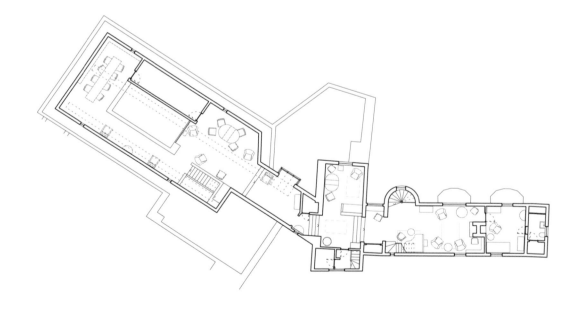

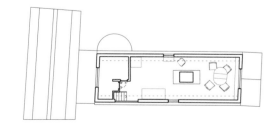

Stephen Marshall
Wiltshire   UK
1998 & 2001
225m²   2,420 sq ft

East Sussex   UK
2013
370m²   3,980 sq ft

Roche Court

Lewes Rectory

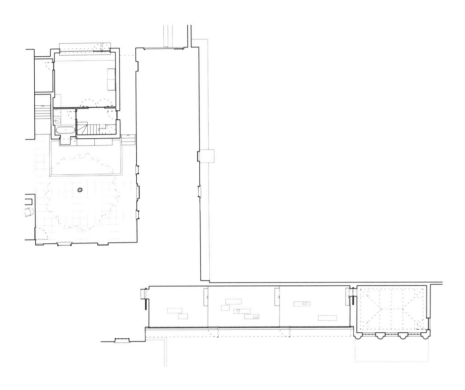

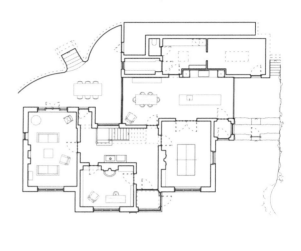

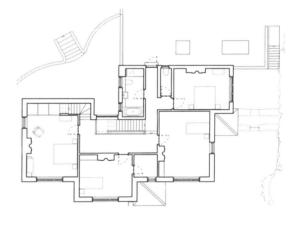

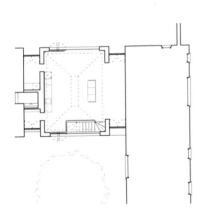

Biographies

William Smalley

William Smalley established his studio in 2010 with the simple aim of making beautiful spaces and places. He has since worked around the UK and abroad. He has been described as an architect of rare sensibility, and his work as having the simplicity of a limewashed medieval building, filtered and made lucid through a completely modern sensibility. This is his first book.

Edmund de Waal

Edmund de Waal is an internationally renowned artist and writer, best known for his large-scale installations of porcelain vessels, often created in response to collections and archives. He published his bestselling family memoir, *The Hare with Amber Eyes*, in 2010. He lives and works in London.

Harry Crowder

Harry Crowder is a British photographer, based in London and working nationally and internationally, focusing on interiors and architecture. His work seeks to capture the feeling of being in a space. He travelled extensively with William in the shooting of this book.

Hélène Binet

Hélène Binet is an internationally acclaimed Swiss–French photographer based in London. She studied photography in Rome, and over more than thirty-five years has captured both contemporary and historic architecture. She is a fervent advocate of analogue photography, working exclusively on film.

Credits

Acknowledgments

Writing a book focuses the memory, and in writing this I have been ever more conscious of the freedom my parents, Catherine and Roger, afforded me to find things out for myself, trust my intuition and allow influences, be it the architecture of twelfth-century Cistercian monks, the music of J. S. Bach or the art of Ben Nicholson.

I owe gratitude to the architects, owners and clients, living and otherwise, who created the places in the book, for having cared enough to make a piece of beauty in the world.

I am grateful to all the clients of the studio who have entrusted their homes to us, and for all those past and present who have worked with me in the studio to bring them to fruition, especially my associate Liam Andrews. The making of this book has been no less a project, and all thanks are due to Scarlett Christie for its being here.

Good friends Jon Moslet & Marco Scire, Melina & Dimitri Blaxland-Horne and Scott Nethersole provided beautiful retreats for the words to be written, and my thanks go to all of them, and also to Ollie Bingham for reading the words on my return.

Greatest of thanks to Harry Crowder for going on this journey with me, and for capturing the soul of the places in your photographs. And to Luke Fenech for bringing beautiful order to these pages. Thanks to Hélène Binet for the poetry of your pictures, and to Edmund de Waal for the poetry of your words.

My thanks to Vincent Van Duysen for making the introduction to Thames & Hudson, and to all there, and especially my editors Lucas Dietrich and Fleur Jones, for their trust and support in creating this book, of which, impossibly it seems as I write, this is the last word.

First published in the United Kingdom in 2023 by
Thames & Hudson Ltd, 181A High Holborn, London WC1V 7QX

First published in the United States of America in 2023 by
Thames & Hudson Inc., 500 Fifth Avenue, New York, New York 10110

British Library Cataloguing-in-Publication Data
A catalogue record for this book is available from the British Library

Library of Congress Control Number 2023935987

ISBN 978-0-500-34369-2
Special edition (not for resale) ISBN 978-0-500-96601-3

Printed and bound in China by C&C Offset Printing Co. Ltd.

Be the first to know about our new releases,
exclusive content and author events by visiting
thamesandhudson.com
thamesandhudsonusa.com
thamesandhudson.com.au